ONE FLEW OVER THE CUCKOO'S NEST

NOTES

Including
- *Life and Background*
- *Introduction*
- *Critical Commentaries*
- *Character Analyses*
- *Special Topics*
- *Review Questions*
- *Selected Bibliography*

by
Thomas R. Holland, Ph.D.
University of Nebraska

Cliffs Notes
INCORPORATED
LINCOLN, NEBRASKA 68501

Editor

Gary Carey, M.A.
University of Colorado

Consulting Editor

James L. Roberts, Ph.D.
Department of English
University of Nebraska

ISBN 0-8220-0962-5
© Copyright 1974
by
Cliffs Notes, Inc.
All Rights Reserved
Printed in U.S.A.

1999 Printing

Cliffs Notes, Inc.   Lincoln, Nebraska

CONTENTS

LIFE AND BACKGROUND

Ken Kesey was born in La Junta, Colorado, in 1935. During his childhood, his family migrated to Oregon, which is the setting of both of his published novels. He was married in 1956, while a student at the University of Oregon, and he received his Bachelor of Arts degree in 1957. His interest in writing led him to the creative writing program at Stanford University. During the period at Stanford, he volunteered for an experimental program at a local Veterans' Administration Hospital to test the effects of newly discovered drugs. Here he discovered LSD and its mind-altering properties. He believed that LSD might be a new tool for going beyond rational consciousness to an entirely new mode of perception, and his interest in states of altered consciousness led him to take a night job in a mental hospital. Here he began to write the first draft of *One Flew Over the Cuckoo's Nest*; several of the characters in the novel are based upon patients in the hospital. He held long conversations with patients, frequently when he was under the influence of drugs himself, in order to gain insight into their particular view of the world. And in the interest of accuracy in the novel, he even persuaded a friend to give him a shock treatment so that he could describe its effects. *One Flew Over the Cuckoo's Nest* is largely a product of Kesey's interest in drugs and insanity, and its effectiveness is, in large part, due to the success with which he has communicated the state of consciousness which he describes as being totally "without preconceptions," particularly in the character of Chief Bromden, the narrator of the book. His second novel, *Sometimes a Great Notion*, is much more conventional, but largely unsuccessful; even its author considers it a disappointment.

With the success of his first novel, Kesey bought a farm outside La Honda, California, where he and his friends began increasingly public experimentations with LSD. He found himself the center of the growing drug cult of the sixties, and he seriously considered drugs a means of altering the world for the better. But with the growing public outcry against drugs, and especially against LSD, Kesey's notoriety led him to trouble, and he fled to Mexico to avoid prosecution. (For a detailed "insider's" account of Kesey's involvement with drugs, the reader is referred to Tom Wolfe's *The Electric Kool-Aid Acid Test*.) After his return to the United States and a short stint of public notoriety, he was sent to jail. He has since been released and now lives quietly with his wife and four children on his family's farm in Oregon. He has recently published a collection of shorter writings, *Ken Kesey's Garage Sale*, and is currently working on another novel.

INTRODUCTION

The setting of *One Flew Over the Cuckoo's Nest* is a mental hospital in Oregon, and the characters, with a few minor exceptions, are all either inmates or employees of this institution. Kesey, following satiric convention, uses the madhouse as a microcosm of American society, a small model of society in which the internal policies reflect the order of the external world.

Kesey gives the reader an insider's view of the hospital by choosing as his narrator one of the patients. The world which this narrator describes is one in which the borders of sanity and insanity are unclear; in fact, he frequently makes it seem that the patients, for all their eccentricities, are really more sane than the authorities who control their lives.

The central figure of the novel is Randle P. McMurphy, a con man who has had himself committed to the hospital in order to escape work at the prison farm, where he was serving a six-month sentence. The story begins with McMurphy's admission to the hospital and ends with his "mercy killing" at the hands of the narrator, Chief Bromden.

In some respects, Bromden is the protagonist of the novel. He begins as a paranoid-schizophrenic, posing as a deaf-mute. He has been on the ward for some fifteen years and knows the workings of the hospital better than any of the other patients. He is drawn to McMurphy, as are all the inmates, and during the course of the novel, the Chief learns from McMurphy who he is, and how to be himself. In effect, he has been "dead" for years and is being brought back to life. His escape at the end of the book is his final resurrection and symbolizes McMurphy's final victory over Nurse Ratched, the "Big Nurse" who is in charge of the ward.

The central conflict of the novel, McMurphy's struggle against the Big Nurse, rapidly takes on overtones of a symbolic battle between the forces of Good and Evil—freedom and individualism, represented by McMurphy, against social authority, conformity and repression, represented by Nurse Ratched. The polarization of these extremes is complete: there are no grey areas, no compromises. Nor does all the action take place at a purely literal level: the Chief's dreams, visions, memories, and fantasies serve to give a heavily symbolic overtone to the story, investing it with elements of myth. To him, the Big Nurse and McMurphy are giants, engaged in a powerful struggle for control over the minds of the patients (though, ironically, he is physically much larger than either McMurphy or the Big Nurse). In effect, the Chief is not so much telling a story as he is creating a myth. And Kesey occasionally plays ironic games with this process of mythmaking. For example, he uses a complex of associations with Melville's novel *Moby-Dick*, another highly symbolic novel which pits good against evil, structure against nature. The only overt reference to the novel is when McMurphy appears on the ward wearing black underwear with pictures of white whales on it. The underwear was a gift from a female literature major at Berkeley: "She said I was a symbol." McMurphy's joke is mildly obscene and intended lightly. But it emphasizes the serious associations with *Moby-Dick*, which Kesey is trying to underscore. With her white uniform and immense size, the Big Nurse resembles Moby Dick, the white whale; like him, she is a terrifying force beyond human control, and she also shares the maniacal sense of guilt which inflicts the whale's opponent, Captain Ahab. But Kesey's myth is much simpler than Melville's multi-layered allegory; here, the lines of good and evil are clearly drawn. (Another token of Kesey's debt to Melville is the character Billy Bibbit, the stuttering innocent whose name and general character were taken from Melville's story "Billy Budd.")

At the beginning of the novel, McMurphy is clearly a self-centered, if attractive, figure. He has had himself diagnosed as psychotic in order to escape the work farm, and once on the ward, he sets out to organize things the way he wants them. He draws the inmates into gambling games, which he inevitably wins, and he tries to make things as comfortable and profitable for himself as possible. But he meets immediate resistance from Nurse Ratched. She runs a tightly organized ward, and troublemakers are strictly dealt with. (The Chief recalls the example of the last such troublemaker, Max Taber, as an example. His attempts to reorganize the ward resulted in his receiving Electro-Shock Treatments. He was ultimately "cured," with a machine installed in his brain, and released from the hospital.)

By the end of the first chapter, McMurphy is clearly challenging the authority of the Big Nurse. He wins a major confrontation over the privilege of watching the World Series on television when he persuades a majority of the patients on the ward to agree with him. The Nurse attempts to demonstrate her authority by cutting off the power to the television set, but the other inmates gather around McMurphy in front of the blank screen in a state of open rebellion.

But before McMurphy's troublemaking becomes serious, he makes an important discovery. Because he was involuntarily committed, he cannot leave the hospital until the staff — primarily the Big Nurse — consider him cured. He has entered into a power struggle in which he holds no real power. Upon learning this, McMurphy begins to conform, but he finds that he has become responsible for the rights of the other patients on the ward. They have become dependent upon him for leadership, and he is no longer able to act only for himself. This becomes clear to him when Cheswick, who had been his main ally among the inmates, drowns himself in despair, and when he learns that the other Acute patients have committed themselves, because *they* consider themselves unfit to live outside the institution. From this point on, McMurphy begins to act in their behalf, trying to give them the freedom he has, to teach them to be themselves.

McMurphy begins by smashing his hand through the glass window of the nurses' station, pretending to be after a pack of cigarettes. Soon the other inmates are joining him in overt acts of rebellion. The Big Nurse finds herself at a disadvantage, but she simply bides her time, waiting for McMurphy to make a mistake.

McMurphy takes advantage of the Big Nurse's passiveness to organize a fishing trip for the inmates, in the company of a prostitute from Portland. The trip is the high point of McMurphy's influence. Outside the hospital and on their own on the open sea, the inmates learn to act for themselves and regain their self-respect. The "rabbits," as Harding described the patients early in the book, are rapidly becoming men.

The Big Nurse realizes that her authority is in serious danger, and after the fishing trip she tries to drive a wedge between McMurphy and his followers. The stratagem she chooses is to emphasize McMurphy's larcenous nature. He has made a profit on the fishing trip by charging each man more than his share, and he has been continually winning from the men in his gambling games since he came on the ward. There is no denying these charges, but Harding defends McMurphy, pointing out that he is, after all, only human and interested in his own welfare. Unfortunately, McMurphy chooses that moment to make a serious mistake. He has undertaken a program of "blowing up" the Chief to his full size — reassuring him of his strength and individuality. The Chief has responded and is now able to lift the bulky control panel on the ward. McMurphy has previously tried to lift the panel on a bet and failed, but now he bets the other patients that the Chief can lift it. The patients, thinking they know the Chief, bet against him and lose. This seems to confirm what the Nurse has been charging against McMurphy, and even Chief Bromden feels that he has been used to con the other patients.

McMurphy is now cornered. The strain of keeping the men on his side, of restoring their self-esteem, has already worn him down. Now he is forced to act again to regain their confidence. The occasion comes later that same day, when one of the orderlies tries to force a reluctant patient, who is terrified of dirt, to have an enema. McMurphy defends George, and the Chief, realizing what McMurphy must do, sides with him. The two win the fight, but are sent to the Disturbed ward to await judgment. There, the Big Nurse confronts them and tries to force an apology. McMurphy refuses and the two are sent to Electro-Shock Therapy.

The Chief is returned to the ward before McMurphy and finds that he has become a legend. He has not spoken to anyone except McMurphy in years, but now he tells the men about McMurphy. No one is surprised to hear him speak. He is accepted and understood. His cure is nearing completion.

When McMurphy returns to the ward, he puts on a good show of being his old self, but the others can see that he is not. The Chief sees a tired resignation in his face, almost desperate. He is waiting to die. And Harding, talking with McMurphy about the pressures of society which have driven the others crazy, tells him that he, too, is now crazy. The strain of his responsibility has been too much for him, and as the patients in his charge grew well, McMurphy became insane in their place. He is mentally unable to go on. When the other inmates arrange his escape, he does not go; he is no longer able to face the outside world.

The escape is arranged for the night of the "party" thrown for Billy Bibbit, who is to lose his virginity to the prostitute Candy Starr, with whom he has fallen in love on the fishing trip. She and another whore sneak onto the ward with bottles of wine and vodka; narcotic cough syrup is stolen from the nurses' station, and the old black watchman, Mr. Turkle, provides a supply of marijuana. Harding realizes the significance of the party; it is the inmates' last fling. There will be no forgiveness for them after this. It is as if McMurphy had chosen to push them to the point of decision. Yet he is unable to escape at the end of the party and is caught in the morning, along with the other inmates.

The Big Nurse places the blame for the disorder on her ward upon McMurphy. At first, the inmates present a united front against her, but she knows their weaknesses. She confronts Billy Bibbit with what his mother will think about what he has done, and he breaks down. While he is left alone in the office, he takes a razor and cuts his throat. The Nurse has aroused all his deep, sensitive shame, and he is unable to live with it.

In one last desperate act, McMurphy attacks Nurse Ratched, tearing open her uniform and attempting to strangle her. He does not kill her, but the exposure of her enormous breasts has exposed her sexuality and effectively destroyed her power over the inmates. They are now free and most of them leave the ward before McMurphy is returned.

When McMurphy is brought back to the ward, he has been lobotomized and is now merely a vegetable. The Chief recognizes that the Nurse wants to use him as a symbol of her continuing authority and he cannot permit this. That night, when he thinks no one is watching, he smothers McMurphy. It is the only way that his victory can be preserved.

Scanlon, who has witnessed the murder, helps Chief Bromden escape from the ward and promises to testify to having seen McMurphy alive after the Chief escaped. The hospital has no policy of attempting to recapture runaways, so it is assumed that the Chief will have no difficulty escaping. He lifts the control panel, as McMurphy taught him, and throws it through the barred window. Then he crawls out into the night and sets off southward, following the path of the flock of wild geese he saw through the window, earlier in the novel.

The Chief's freedom is an emblem of McMurphy's victory. He has "been away a long time," both literally and symbolically. For he is an Indian, the "noble savage," the "vanishing American" who is about to reappear. McMurphy's rejection of the forms of "civilized" behavior has given Bromden a new life. And though McMurphy has failed personally (and, symbolically, his hat is too small for the Chief when he

tries it on at the end of the novel), he has succeeded in "resur-
recting" the Chief and the other inmates.

Yet there are hints in the novel that the conclusion cannot
be termed a total victory for McMurphy's followers. One such
hint is the discrepancy in the narration at the beginning of the
first part, which may be read to imply that the Chief has been
recaptured and brought back to the ward, where his paranoia
has returned. Consider, too, the fact that the Chief sets off "in
the direction I remembered seeing the dog go, toward the
highway"; this links his fate with that of the dog, which was
headed toward certain destruction. Yet such inconsistencies
and ambiguities must be considered as undercurrents, for the
novel closes in an optimistic tone, and the reader is left with
the clear impression that, despite the dangers, the Chief will
escape and will succeed in his new life.

LIST OF CHARACTERS

Randle P. McMurphy

A manual laborer, gambler and con man, who is admitted to the ward from Pendleton Prison Farm, diagnosed as a psychotic. Really not insane, he transforms the ward by teaching the other inmates how to be free. Finally lobotomized after attacking Nurse Ratched, he is killed in his sleep by Chief Bromden.

Nurse Ratched

The "Big Nurse," a representative of the "Combine," the Chief's name for the forces of repressive organization in society. She is a former Army nurse, in her fifties — an absolute tyrant. She maintains order by pitting the inmates against one another; McMurphy compares her techniques with the "brainwashing" used by the Communists during the Korean conflict.

Chief Bromden

A huge paranoid-schizophrenic Indian, the narrator of the novel. He is a Chronic, diagnosed as incurable, and has been on the ward since the end of World War II. He imagines himself to be small and weak and pretends to be a deaf-mute in order to protect himself. The Chief is gradually rehabilitated by McMurphy and emerges as the real protagonist of the book at the end. He kills McMurphy after the Big Nurse has had him lobotomized, and escapes from the hospital.

Dale Harding

An effeminate man, psychologically "castrated" by his wife, who has committed himself to the hospital.

Billy Bibbit

A frightened thirty-one-year-old man with the mind of an adolescent. He is dominated by his mother, who is a friend of Nurse Ratched.

Max Taber

A former patient who caused Nurse Ratched trouble. He was dismissed after being made docile by Electro-Shock Therapy.

Scanlon

A patient with destructive fantasies. The last of McMurphy's followers left on the ward, he assists in the Chief's escape after McMurphy's death.

Cheswick

McMurphy's most overt follower in his early days on the ward. After McMurphy begins to yield to authority, Cheswick drowns himself.

Martini

Exists in a world of delusions; his visions are more real to him than reality.

Seefeld and Frederickson

Epileptics. Seefeld refuses to take his medicine; Frederickson takes double dosages.

Big George (Rub-A-Dub)

A former seaman with a morbid fear of dirt. He is captain of the boat on the fishing trip, and his fear of an enema ignites the fight between McMurphy and the Chief and the black boys.

The Lifeguard

A former football player who has been committed to the hospital. He explains to McMurphy that commitment means that McMurphy can be released only when the Big Nurse agrees.

Tadem and Gregory

Two Acutes who join the fishing excursion.

Pete Bancini

A patient who, like McMurphy, was "missed" by the Combine, but suffered permanent brain damage at birth. He tells the other patients that he was "born dead."

Colonel Matterson

A "wheeler," confined permanently to a wheelchair. He raves continually in disconnected metaphors.

Ellis

Entered the hospital as an Acute, but was mistakenly given too much Electro-Shock Therapy. Stands permanently "crucified" against the wall.

Ruckly

Another mistake, an Acute made Chronic by over-use of EST.

Old Rawler

A noisy patient in Disturbed; castrates himself and bleeds to death.

Old Blastic

A "vegetable"; dies in his sleep during the Chief's dream of the mechanized butcher shop.

Doctor Spivey

A morphine addict, chosen by the Big Nurse to work on her ward because of his weakness and vulnerability.

Nurse with a Birthmark

Terrified of the patients, especially of McMurphy. A Catholic, she seems to be driven by her sense of guilt and fear of sex.

Japanese Nurse

Works on Disturbed; criticizes the extreme methods of Nurse Ratched.

The "Black Boys" (Washington, Warren, and Geever)

Chosen by the Big Nurse as orderlies because of their hostility and strength. They keep order on the ward mainly by threatening the patients.

Mr. Turkle

An elderly Negro who works as an orderly at night. He is bribed by McMurphy to arrange the "party" for Candy and Billy Bibbit.

Candy Starr

A prostitute from Portland; a "whore with a heart of gold." Billy Bibbit falls in love with her on the fishing trip.

Sandy Gilfilliam

Candy's friend; comes with her to the party on the ward.

Captain Block

Captain of the fishing boat stolen by the inmates.

CRITICAL COMMENTARIES

PART 1

The first section of this novel, the longest of the four parts, is devoted primarily to setting the scene in which almost all of the subsequent action will take place, and putting into motion the main conflict of the novel. The setting is a mental hospital in Oregon, and the characters, with a few exceptions, are either inmates or employees of this institution. In his opening chapter, Kesey establishes the setting, introduces and develops all the main characters, and leads the reader into the central conflict which will dominate the rest of the novel—the contest of wills between McMurphy and the Big Nurse, Nurse Ratched. The world depicted in the novel is divided into two parts, polarized about the individuals which represent them. Symbolically, McMurphy is the "natural man," representing freedom, unrestrained sexuality, and rugged individualism; the Big Nurse is mechanized civilization at its worst—sexual repression and mass conformity. The novel concerns the conflict of freedom and restriction in the competition between McMurphy and Nurse Ratched, with the other characters as mere pawns caught up in the struggle. It is abundantly clear from the first that the author stands firmly on McMurphy's side; McMurphy is working to free his fellow patients, whereas the Big Nurse is working to keep them submissive to the will of the "Combine," the forces of repressive civilization which she represents.

One of the book's most effective devices is the author's choice of a narrator. Third-person, objective narration is abandoned in favor of choosing a spokesman from among the inmates who witnesses, and eventually participates in, McMurphy's struggle with the Combine. The narrator is not an ordinary inmate; he is a large, powerful, paranoid-schizophrenic Indian, who has already been one of the primary victims of the Combine. Chief Bromden is a half-breed, the child of an Indian father and a white mother. The fact that he has taken his mother's name, rather than his father's Indian name, is an image of his subjection to the forces of white civilization, the forces of female domination over male freedom.

The Chief is particularly effective as a narrator because of his pretense of being a deaf-mute. In the early parts of the novel, he plays the role of a passive observer, merely reporting what he sees, taking little part in the action. Because he is believed to be deaf and dumb, he is permitted to see and hear things which are concealed from the other inmates. When, as the novel progresses, the Chief begins to get involved in the action, his progress toward a "cure" is the clearest indication that McMurphy's radical "therapy" has been working for the patients. What we have, in effect, is a narrator who begins the story as a well-informed, passive observer, and ends by being a principal participant in the action.

But the Chief presents some unique problems as a narrator; he is, in fact, insane. His paranoia is clear in the first sentence of the book: "They're out there." All the Chief's perceptions, especially in this first chapter, are colored by his paranoia, and this makes it difficult for the reader, at times, to sort out fact from fantasy. But the Chief's disease is nothing more than a function of the way he has been treated by the Combine, by female-dominated white civilization. And the lurid fantasies he indulges in are symbolic representations of the world as he sees it. His delusions are, in effect, images of the way his mind apprehends the workings of reality.

To the Chief, his images tend to fall into associative groups, and the images of his fantasies become central symbols in the book. The majority of his delusions are associated with machines of various kinds, and the machine is the very image of the structured, female-dominated society which McMurphy is fighting against. The Big Nurse, when angry, is described in terms of a diesel truck running out of control. Her gestures are described as "automatic," mechanical rather than natural. The name the Chief chooses to designate organized society, the "Combine," is the name of a machine used to thresh wheat.

The most important of the machines is the "fog machine," which the Big Nurse uses to keep control on the ward. When things begin to get out of hand, she turns on the war-surplus fog machine in the walls (Chief Bromden saw similar machines in Europe during World War II), and everyone becomes lost in the fog. The fog machine is a particularly effective device in the novel because it corresponds with the state of the Chief's paranoia. It is when he is at his worst that the fog rolls in; later in the novel, as he begins to recover, the fog disappears completely.

The Chief's association of machines with the forces of repression seems to be related with the destruction of his tribe by the construction of a hydroelectric dam on their land. This was the first contact with the forces of mechanization; the building of the dam was what ruined his father, causing him to "shrink," as his mother began to dominate the family. The Chief's most vivid fantasy of mechanization, the butcher shop in which carcasses of dead inmates are strung up like sides of beef, is akin to his ideas about the dam. The fantasy begins with a humming sound, much like electric transformers at a dam; the ward is lowered directly into the depths of the dam, where the Chief sees the machinery and the corpses. This particular fantasy is made more horrible by the fact that it is related to reality: when the Chief awakens from his dream, he finds that Old Blastic, one of the "vegetables," died during the night. The corpse which the Chief saw on the meat hook was Blastic's.

The dam is also the source of electricity, and electricity is, both symbolically and literally, another of the tools the Big Nurse has at her disposal in keeping order on the ward. At the beginning of the chapter, the Chief has a vision of Nurse Ratched as a huge white spider at the middle of a web of electric wires, controlling the machines installed in the walls. Electricity is literally used in the "Shock Shop" to administer Electro-Shock Therapy (EST) to unruly patients. The Chief himself has undergone some two hundred sessions of EST (he mentions that it was always in the fog that he found his way to the Shock Shop). And EST, along with the machines he imagines in the walls, is a major element in the Chief's paranoia.

During Electro-Shock Therapy, the patient is strapped onto a table which resembles a cross, and one inmate, Ellis, who has had too much electricity, stands "nailed to the wall" with his arms outspread in the image of a crucified Christ. This image in the first chapter foreshadows later developments in the book as McMurphy, seeing that he must sacrifice himself in order to free his fellow patients, becomes increasingly associated with Christ.

In this first section, the Chief's perceptions tend to emphasize the Combine's views of himself and his fellow patients. Going along with the views of society, he describes the other Chronics as "broken machines"; the inmates, in fact, describe the hospital as a "repair shop," where misfits are sent to be adjusted to fit into society.

Another disarrangement of the Chief's perception has to do with his physical size. Despite his real size and strength, he imagines himself to be small and weak, and he sees the smaller McMurphy and Nurse Ratched as gigantic individuals who are engaged in a mythic battle with one another. In effect, he is able to see the stores of strength within others and he translates this into a distortion of their size. The Big Nurse is "big" because she has enormous power over the others; McMurphy is big because he dares defy the Big Nurse.

It is this controlled universe that McMurphy enters when he has himself committed to avoid work on the prison farm, and it is evident from the first, even to the other inmates, that he does not fit into this world. He resists the efforts of the Big

Nurse and her orderlies, the black boys, to keep him in line. He is friendly and outgoing toward the other patients, able to laugh and sing (unlike the other inmates, who can barely manage to snicker occasionally into their fists when no one is looking). Above all, McMurphy is able to accept the others for what they are and to see through their pretenses into their true natures as individuals. It is precisely his ability to be an individual, and to see the others as individuals, that constitutes McMurphy's threat to the order imposed by the Combine. The Big Nurse's system works by a kind of enforced paranoia. Inmates are encouraged to attack one another's weaknesses in Group Therapy meetings and to inform on one another in the log book kept on the ward. Thus everyone is a potential enemy, part of the forces conspiring to keep the inmate in line. In this situation, everyone must conform in order to avoid punishment.

McMurphy's staunch refusal to conform quickly leads him to a confrontation with the Big Nurse, and the outcome of this confrontation is foreshadowed early in the first section in the Chief's memories of Max Taber. Taber was another misfit who made trouble for the Big Nurse. But she eventually subdued him by using EST and he was forced to conform. In fact, his "therapy" was so successful that he could be released to the outside world. He was "cured," but his cure was the substitution of one of the Combine's machines for his personality. He was a prime example of a "broken machine" undergoing repair. With reference to Taber's case, the Chief says that the hospital is "a factory for the Combine. It's for fixing up mistakes made in the neighborhoods and in the schools and in the churches, the hospital is." Those who will not conform are sent there for repair. Some, like the Chief, are "broken" machines; these are the Chronics, who are doomed to spend the rest of their lives in the institution. But the Acutes are presumably there to be helped, to be adjusted to conform to the rules of the Combine and sent back out into society.

Even among the Acutes, McMurphy is an exception. Most of the others have been subject to the Combine all their lives and are used to operating within its confines. They have come to the ward, most of them voluntarily committed, because of their own sense of guilt at their inability to conform completely. But McMurphy is one of those rare individuals whom the Combine has somehow missed. He has managed to be what he is, to retain his individuality, and to resist the encroachments of social authority.

It is clear from the moment he is admitted that McMurphy is on a collision course with the Big Nurse. But the actual confrontation builds slowly. He does provoke her with his comments at his admission, and at the beginning of the Group Therapy meeting, but then he quiets down and watches the meeting. Later, in discussing the meeting with the other patients, he describes it as a "pecking party" in a chicken yard. First, one chicken is bloodied, then the others encourage one another to peck freely at his wound. As he is pecked to pieces, others are splattered with his blood, and they in turn become victims. His implication is clear: the Big Nurse is using the inmates to destroy one another. The meetings are not therapeutic—they are destructive. He tells Harding the purpose of the "pecking": she is out to castrate them, to rob them of their manhood and individuality. Even the doctor she has chosen for the ward, Dr. Spivey, is under her control. He was chosen because of his drug addiction, and the Big Nurse uses the threat of blackmail to keep him "castrated."

McMurphy's method of dealing with the other inmates is in direct contrast to the Big Nurse's. Whereas she forces them to concentrate upon their weaknesses, he concentrates upon their strengths. And whereas she attempts to castrate them, he emphasizes their masculinity. His first conversation with Harding emphasizes this point: McMurphy challenges Harding to an insanity contest in order to determine who is the "chief bullgoose loony." (The irony of the term "bullgoose" is compounded by Harding's apparent effeminacy.) And he teases Billy Bibbit about his legendary sexual adventures. He refuses to see the patients as "rabbits," as they see themselves.

Though McMurphy does become the leader of the inmates, his primary aim is to teach them how to lead themselves. At first he does this unconsciously, acting primarily out of self-interest. The gambling area is set up because McMurphy wants it, and he freely admits that his primary purpose is to win whatever he can from the other patients. But his victories are their victories as well, and he begins to be seen — both by the others and by himself — as their leader.

McMurphy's first open conflict with the Big Nurse, his second day on the ward, concerns gambling on the ward. The piped-in music is too loud to suit him, and the Nurse refuses to let the men play cards in the tub room. Surprisingly, Dr. Spivey sides with McMurphy: some of McMurphy's spirit is beginning to affect him. Once the issue of the tub room is set, McMurphy refuses to let the Big Nurse dominate her usual group meeting. *He* dominates the rest of the meeting by discussing a made-up "dream" of his own in order to keep attention away from the other patients.

McMurphy has won the first round and has demonstrated to the others the seriousness of his bet that he can defeat the Big Nurse. But the Chief recognizes that the victory is only temporary. As he looks at the Big Nurse, she seems to swell up and fill the whole end of the room. She is too big to be beaten; she must win in the end. Recognizing this fact, the Chief again retreats into the fog. He is still unable to face the real situation; he must withdraw into himself.

The other patients apparently begin to share the Chief's belief that McMurphy cannot win. During a group meeting later in the week, McMurphy asks for a vote on whether they will watch the World Series on television; only Cheswick and Scanlon are willing to back him. None of the other inmates fully trust McMurphy, for he has been winning all their money and cigarettes while gambling with them. They recognize that he is looking out primarily for his own interests, and they do not believe they have anything to gain by siding with him. But McMurphy finds a device with which to win their confidence. In discussing the possibility of escaping the ward to watch the World Series at a tavern, he bets all his previous winnings that he can lift a huge control panel (the escape plan is to throw it through the grill over the window and escape out the window). He loses the bet, of course. But he has demonstrated his good faith; the others are now more willing to take his side.

This episode of lifting the control panel foreshadows later events in the book. In part, what McMurphy is doing in this scene is losing one bet in order to set up a later, more lucrative bet. McMurphy's rehabilitation of Chief Bromden back to his full size is proven to be complete when the Chief can lift the control panel, and McMurphy, having secretly tested the Chief's ability for himself, bets the other patients that he can. The plan to escape from the hospital by throwing the panel through the window is used by the Chief at the end of the novel, after he has killed McMurphy. In effect, by demonstrating his own limitations, McMurphy has challenged the others to surpass him.

Part 1 ends with another group meeting, during which another vote is taken on the World Series issue. After McMurphy's loss of the first vote, the Big Nurse believes herself to be back in firm control, and the Chief is slipping deeper and deeper into the fog as the meeting progresses. The meeting is suddenly interrupted when Billy Bibbit, whose problem is being discussed, can no longer stand the pressure and walks out. McMurphy seizes upon this opportunity to bring up the vote again. The Acutes side with McMurphy this time, but the Nurse refuses to concede defeat. She insists that the Chronics' votes must also count—and none of them have raised their hands. McMurphy is one vote short. While the Big Nurse is attempting to adjourn the meeting, sure of her victory, McMurphy approaches Chief Bromden. The Chief does not want to raise his hand; to do so is to voluntarily leave the security of the fog and become vulnerable. But he is unable to control himself. He feels that McMurphy has some curious power over him. His hand raises—as if by itself—and McMurphy wins the vote.

The Big Nurse is unwilling to concede. When McMurphy goes to the television set to watch the game, she cuts off the power. It is clearly a contest of wills, and McMurphy will not give in. He sits in front of the blank screen, ignoring the Nurse's warnings, while the other patients gradually gather around him. At the end of the chapter, the patients are grouped in front of the television set, the Nurse screaming at them from behind to obey her. Chief Bromden observes that if anyone saw them, "they'd of thought the whole bunch was crazy as loons."

The battle between McMurphy and Nurse Ratched is now seriously underway; the other patients have had their first taste of open rebellion. But it is still primarily a contest between individuals; McMurphy has not yet begun to speak for the patients as a group. In this introductory section, his goals in challenging authority have been mainly personal, but as the book progresses, he is forced to set his own interests aside and to act on behalf of the others.

PART 2

The major turning point of the book occurs in the second part. McMurphy's struggles with the authority of the Big Nurse in Part 1 and the early parts of Part 2 are random, self-centered, and ultimately not too serious. He is simply trying to make life on the ward more livable for himself. And, as the Chief learns in the staff meeting early in the second part, Mc-Murphy's success to this point has been only illusory. He has been winning only because the Big Nurse has permitted it; she has decided rather than send him to Disturbed, which would be an admission of her inability to control him, to keep him on the ward and fight it out. She is confident that she will win, precisely because she understands that McMurphy is not seriously deranged. Because his commitment was involuntary, the only circumstances under which McMurphy will be permitted to leave the hospital are the recommendation of the Big Nurse and her staff that he has been cured. Nurse Ratched believes that once he understands that, he will submit to her will.

A little later in the chapter, McMurphy discovers the terms of his commitment; once he has accepted them, he begins to act as the Big Nurse has predicted. Any rebellion on his part would be, literally, a struggle to the death with authority. Furthermore, such a struggle can no longer be self-motivated. Survival dictates conformity in this situation, and any overt rebellion must be sparked by some purpose stronger than personal comfort. Toward the end of this section, Mc-Murphy discovers both his own vulnerability and the reasons for continued resistance.

This section begins with a continuation of the scene in the television room. McMurphy has dispelled the fog in the Chief's mind, and, for the first time, the Chief begins to hope that a permanent change on the ward is possible. But this hope is quickly dispelled when he goes to the staff meeting to clean the room while the meeting is in progress. (He fancies himself to be wiping up bucketfuls of green slime, the product of the evil work that goes on in the room.) The staff, guessing at the Big Nurse's wishes, want to send McMurphy to the Disturbed ward; they feel that he has become an excessively disruptive influence upon the other patients. To everyone's surprise, the Nurse disagrees: she insists that McMurphy is only a normal patient and can be dealt with by the usual methods. Her meaning is clear: she intends to combat McMurphy's influence directly, rather than conceding defeat by sending him to another ward. She tells the staff why she will win eventually. McMurphy is under her care until she decides that he is cured. Time is on her side because the final decision about his fate must come from her, and she is counting upon his rationality to lead him to voluntarily conform with her wishes.

McMurphy, however, is not yet aware of his precarious situation. He continues to dominate the ward, as the Big Nurse holds back, awaiting her opportunity. During this period, the other patients begin to follow McMurphy more openly; they begin to participate in his rebellion. Now, the Chief begins to discern what it is that makes McMurphy so powerful: he is able to be what he is. He is able to retain his individuality and to insist upon it despite authority. Looking in the mirror, the Chief contrasts himself with McMurphy, wondering "how it was possible that anybody could manage such an enormous thing as being what he was." Like the other patients, the Chief has never been able to manage this feat for himself. Although he is six feet seven inches tall, and powerfully built, he sees himself as small and weak—because he is small and weak inside. Ironically, he wonders at McMurphy's size and strength, even though McMurphy is much smaller than himself. For example, during the scene at the swimming pool, the Chief observes that McMurphy must be over a hole in the bottom of the pool, because he has to tread water while the Chief is standing on the bottom. Chief Bromden is still incapable of recognizing reality, of realizing that he is as strong as anyone. His attachment to McMurphy is, at this point, only a part of his delusion of weakness, a function of his disease.

One night, unable to sleep (he has refused to take a sleeping pill), the Chief observes an apparently trivial incident which comes to carry a rather heavy symbolic burden in the book. He is standing, looking out the window on the ward, and sees a dog hunting gophers in the lawn. Suddenly, the dog stands still, listening. A flight of wild geese is flying south for the winter. The Chief watches them as they fly overhead in a "V"; the leader (the "bullgoose," in McMurphy's terminology) momentarily forms a black cross against the moon. Then they are out of sight, and the dog sets off to follow them. Just before the orderlies seize him from behind, the Chief notices that the dog is heading for the highway, and a car is coming. The dog and the car are aimed for the same spot in the road.

The end of this incident is not described for the reader; the Chief is led off to bed before he sees it. But the inevitable outcome is suggested. The dog and the car, the natural and the mechanical, will collide on the road—and the machine, as always, will emerge victorious.

The wild goose represents the untrammeled force of freedom in nature, which the Chief discerns in McMurphy. His fight over the hospital (the "cuckoo's nest" of the title) is merely part of his participation in the ebb and flow of natural forces which guide him south in the winter, north in the summer. But his example inspires the "domestic" animal, the dog, who is caught up partly by the forces of nature, partly by the forces of civilization. The dog's attempt to emulate the goose, to follow him, leads to his destruction by a machine, a product of civilization. This incident is a symbolic warning of the toll exacted by civilization upon those who participate in it. Only by being wild, by being completely apart from civilization, can one be truly free.

It is a few days after this incident that McMurphy learns of the terms of his commitment. The lifeguard at the swimming pool is in the same situation, and he explains to McMurphy that since he was committed, he must remain in the hospital until the staff—and in McMurphy's case, the Big Nurse—decide that he is ready to be discharged. Faced with the seriousness of his situation, McMurphy begins to reassess his behavior and begins to cooperate with the Nurse, as she predicted. He had had himself committed in order to escape work at the prison farm, but he had not bargained on an indefinite stay in the hospital. The Big Nurse's smug prediction in the staff meeting was accurate because she realized that McMurphy would act in his own best interests. Now that he realizes that conformity is in his best interest, McMurphy begins to conform.

But the other inmates are not satisfied with McMurphy's change in behavior. His rebellion has aroused their own long-stifled feelings of dissatisfaction with the ward and they have come to look upon him as their leader. They can understand his sudden instinct for self-preservation, but within themselves, they cannot accept it. This fact is indicated most clearly by Cheswick's suicide. Cheswick had been McMurphy's most open follower; now when he voices his dissatisfaction with ward policies, McMurphy will not even back him. Thus, the next time the inmates are taken swimming, Cheswick swims to the bottom of the pool, seizes the iron grate, and will not let go. Despite McMurphy's attempt to rescue him, he is drowned. Kesey makes the import of the suicide clear by having it occur in the place where McMurphy made his decision to submit. The other inmates, inspired by McMurphy's former example, are no longer willing to accept the status quo. For McMurphy, the solution is simple—submit to authority and be released. For the others, things are not so clear-cut.

After Cheswick's suicide, McMurphy begins to learn more about the complexities of his decision and how it affects the other patients. For instance, he discovers that the two epileptics on the ward, Frederickson and Seefeld, have no viable choice whatever. If they refuse to take their medicine, like Seefeld, they are subject to unpredictable fits, which have the same effect as Electro-Shock Therapy. (In fact, EST was devised after a psychologist noticed the calming effects of shock on an epileptic's subsequent behavior.) But if they do take their medicine, their gums rot and their teeth fall out. Either way, they lose. Unlike McMurphy, they have no clear alternatives.

Shortly after this revelation, Harding's wife pays a visit to the ward. She is an extremely domineering woman, contemptuous of Harding's effeminacy. It is clear that her dominance is largely responsible for Harding's frailty; she is simply another version of the Big Nurse, the castrating female. So, in effect, Harding has no choice: in the hospital or outside, he is subject to the same influences.

As his comprehension of the other inmates' situation grows, McMurphy becomes increasingly irritable and he begins to have nightmares. The nightmares, he says, consist of "faces" — the faces of the other men on the ward. He has begun to recognize his responsibility for them, but he cannot see any way of fulfilling it.

It is also during this period that Harding explains to McMurphy the purpose of the hospital in the Combine's scheme of things. He describes the process of Electro-Shock Therapy as "brain burning" (with a humorous reference to Faulkner's story "Barn Burning") and points out that it is a cure only in the sense that it alters the individual into what society wants him to be. Again, it is the subjection of man to the mass, the opposite of the individualism that McMurphy represents. Lobotomy, the ultimate cure, is a more extreme version of the same process. Harding, sounding more like McMurphy than himself, describes it as "frontal-lobe castration" — the removal of that part of the brain which makes an individual unique, expressed in sexual terms. These are the techniques employed by the Combine in enforcing its will, and McMurphy is now beginning to realize that in submitting to the Big Nurse, he is acquiescing in the use of these weapons against all he stands for. He is beginning to see himself as a leader, as a symbol of the inmates' right to their own individuality. Ironically, in doing so he is beginning to lose his own right to choose for himself.

The real key to McMurphy's realization is his understanding that it is not only the Big Nurse whom he is fighting, but society itself, the Combine, of which she is only one representative. He has already been toying with the half-joking suggestion that raping the Big Nurse would be enough to set things right. By raping her, he would establish her identity as a woman (of which her large breasts, which she tries to conceal, are an image). If she were the only enemy, perhaps this demonstration of masculine dominance would be enough, but she is not.

The final thing that leads McMurphy to his decision to fight back is the disclosure that his situation is unique on the ward. The other Acutes have been voluntarily committed; they are in the hospital because they have chosen to be there, and they are free to leave whenever they wish. They have chosen *not* to fight the Combine, but to submit to it—to have themselves "repaired" in order to fit back into society. The situation is extremely ironic: the other patients have the choice of remaining in society, but not the nerve to do so. McMurphy has the nerve, but not the choice. McMurphy's decision to renew the conflict at the end of this section is made, not for himself, but on behalf of the other patients. In making their choice for them, he is beginning to give them some of his courage. He is embarking upon his own program of therapy, which is bound to end in his own destruction. But its purpose is to free the others by making them able to live in society again, on their own terms.

Meanwhile, McMurphy's period of submission has given the Big Nurse renewed confidence, and she has begun to flaunt her power by revoking more of the inmates' privileges. She has begun a campaign to restore the ward to the order it had before McMurphy's admission, and one of her main symbols of her victory over McMurphy is to be the removal of the patients' privilege of using the tub room for gambling.

The Chief, knowing that McMurphy is about to act, feels the tension in the air. He describes the ringing in his brain, which he used to hear before football games, in anticipation of the opening kickoff. The ringing always stopped with the kickoff, when the game began.

The scene is described in the best tradition of western movies: McMurphy is the gunfighter, striding down the street for the showdown. He walks to the window of the nurses' station and intentionally smashes his hand through the glass to take a pack of his cigarettes, which the Big Nurse had begun to hold in reserve in order to discourage gambling. The battle is begun once more, and the ringing in the Chief's mind has stopped.

PART 3

In the third section of the novel, McMurphy seems to be winning his battle with the Big Nurse. He has had his way on the ward, bringing the other patients, and even the weak Doctor Spivey, onto his side. But Nurse Ratched is simply biding her time, awaiting her opportunity. She may be losing a few battles, but she still has no doubts about her ability to win the war. She seems to know that McMurphy is bound to make himself vulnerable sooner or later. Even he himself appears to have an increasing sense throughout this section that his time is running out.

It is in this part that McMurphy works his miracle upon the other inmates of the ward, bringing them to share in his strength. But it is as if his strength were a fixed quantity; as the others grow stronger, he in turn grows weaker. Increasingly, Chief Bromden notices that McMurphy looks worn out from his efforts, as the other men are becoming stronger and livelier.

McMurphy's breaking the window in the nurses' station, which signalled the beginning of the battle, caught the Big Nurse by surprise. She is able to offer only token resistance to him, and McMurphy seizes the advantage to consolidate his power. Nurse Ratched attempts to punish the inmates by taking away their right to play basketball, but Doctor Spivey, "flexing his muscles" for the first time, sides with McMurphy and the team remains. McMurphy uses the games with staff members as occasions to rough up the large, strong black orderlies in order to assert his defiance of authority even further. And his assertiveness gets more and more brazen: First, he requests an unaccompanied pass to be with Candy Starr, "a twitch I know from Portland." The request is rejected, of course, but McMurphy later follows up with a proposal that the patients be permitted to go on a fishing trip with two of his "aunts" — who turn out to be none other than Candy

Starr and another whore from Portland. The Big Nurse's only defense against this proposal is to prey upon the inmates' fears, with clippings about storms at sea. But she is bound to lose this round because McMurphy's daredevil spirit has become infectious, and the other patients are losing their fears.

Meanwhile, the other patients are beginning to assert themselves on their own, following McMurphy's example. Billy Bibbit has quit informing on the others in the Big Nurse's log book; Harding, discovering his masculinity, has begun to flirt with the student nurses; and Scanlon, when a new window has just been installed in the nurses' station after McMurphy has broken it out again, throws a basketball through it "accidentally." Even Chief Bromden has begun to come back to life. The fog has now lifted permanently, and he feels, against his better judgment, that he wants to join in the fishing trip with McMurphy and the others.

The thought of the fishing trip causes the Chief to remember his childhood, when his tribesmen used to spear salmon from the falls on the Columbia. He is now able to face the truth of his own situation for the first time; he remembers when he first began to feel small, when people first refused to recognize his existence. It occurred when two white men and a woman came to negotiate with his father about building a hydroelectric dam on the river. They talked with one another about the Indians as if the Chief were not present, and they decided that, instead of negotiating with his father, they would use his white mother as a means of getting their way. The Chief then remembers what happened to his father as a result of this decision—how his mother came to dominate the situation; how she "grew big" while his father shrunk and finally became a hopeless alcoholic on the streets of the town. He feels that in damming the river with their machines, and running the tribe away from its home, the white men were also installing machines in his father to make him obey the Combine. And as surely as the machines destroyed his father, they will destroy McMurphy.

The Chief's major breakthrough occurs the night of this memory, when one of the orderlies is scraping the Chief's gum from the bottom of his bed. McMurphy, who has long suspected that the Chief could hear and speak, teases him about saving his chewed gum and finally offers him a stick of fresh Juicy Fruit. Much to his own surprise, the Chief thanks him; it is the first time he has spoken in years. The words come tumbling out. He feels he must warn McMurphy by telling him what the Combine did to his father. In the course of his warning, he tells McMurphy how he has been "shrunk," and McMurphy promises to "blow him back up" to size. But Mc-Murphy makes a miscalculation at this time which will eventually prove to be fatal. He has not entirely abandoned his larcenous ways, for to do so would be untrue to his nature and defeat his whole purpose. Remembering his earlier bet about lifting the control panel, he sees a way to make some money, so he asks the Chief to promise that when he is full-sized again, he will prove his strength by lifting the control panel for him. This promise eventually provides the Big Nurse with just the Achilles' heel she has been looking for.

During the conversation, the Chief feels himself gaining strength, just from talking to McMurphy. He feels he wants to touch him, but is ashamed of the impulse because of its homosexual overtones. Yet he knows that he just wants to touch McMurphy "because he's a man . . . because he's who he is." The Chief also notices one of McMurphy's tattoos—a poker hand, aces and eights. This is the so-called dead man's hand, the hand which Wild Bill Hickok was supposedly holding when he was murdered. The notice of this tattoo at this point in the book (it has been mentioned before, but not dwelt upon in any detail) serves to foreshadow what is in store for McMurphy and to underscore the Chief's warnings.

McMurphy persuades the Chief to go fishing with the group and signs his name to the list. The next morning, the day of the trip, the Chief refuses to accept the broom from the orderly; he has made his decision and it would be beneath his dignity to submit now to the menial chores customarily

38

assigned to him. McMurphy, meanwhile, finds the last member of his crew — Big George, an old Swedish fisherman who is reluctant to go along because the boats are too "dirty." George has a phobia about dirt, which will later figure in McMurphy's downfall.

The patients, somewhat influenced by the Big Nurse's warnings about the dangers of the sea, are somewhat apprehensive about their adventure, but once Candy Starr arrives, all fear is forgotten. Her sexuality is strongly contrasted with the "sterility" of the nurses. As she enters the ward, the Chief sees the machines in the walls "committing suicide," unable to compete with the strength of her natural forces. Even Billy Bibbit, the most rabbit-like of the inmates, is aroused to whistle at her.

As the crew prepares to go, Kesey begins to develop the religious imagery in association with McMurphy. Ellis, from his "crucified" position on the wall, tells the patients to be "fishers of men," the phrase used by Christ to persuade the fishermen Peter and Andrew to follow him. (Billy, looking at Candy, says, "To hell with the fishers of *men* business!" He is making remarkable progress.) And as McMurphy leads his crew into the outside world and toward the sea, the Chief notes that there are twelve followers — like Christ's twelve disciples. This imagery is used again and is reinforced in the last chapter.

Once outside the hospital, the patients become aware of how much the world has changed in their absence. Chief Bromden, especially, notices how the machines have come to dominate everything. But the group gains strength from McMurphy's example. An unpleasant confrontation at a gas station gives them a sense of power, and Harding even proposes the formation of a pressure group, the NAAIP (National Association for the Advancement of Insane People, based upon the NAACP) to lobby for lunatics' rights. His image of a babbling schizophrenic manning a wrecking machine fits nicely into the Chief's fantasies—turning the machine upon itself, destroying the Combine with its own tools.

But the inmates' power is still fragile. When another confrontation arises with the captain of the boat, and McMurphy leaves the group to discuss the matter with him in the bait shop, the other patients find themselves unable to cope with the insults of the loafers on the dock. The Chief realizes how weak they still are: "We weren't fit to be out here with people." The whole expedition threatens to be a failure, to reinforce the patients' sense of insecurity. But McMurphy saves the situation. When the captain refuses to let them take the boat, he lures him away from the group, and steals it. George is made captain (a wise decision, since he is the only one of the group who knows anything about the sea), and they are off.

Once they begin to catch fish, the men find to their surprise that they can cope. McMurphy spends the first part of the trip below with Candy, leaving the men to their own devices. And when the fish begin to strike and chaos erupts on deck, he stands off to one side, laughing, not lifting a hand to help. The other patients no longer need his help; they are acting on their own. The Chief sees the pain McMurphy is undergoing; the experience has been a tremendous drain on his own strength. But he is still able to laugh: "...he won't let the *pain* blot out the humor no more'n he'll let the humor blot out the pain."

While the doctor is attempting to land a large flounder, a storm comes up, and there are not enough life vests to go around. But McMurphy is not among the "heroes" who volunteer to risk their lives; he intentionally fades into the background. Instead, Billy, Harding, and George forego the vests. George refuses because the vests, like everything else in life, are too "dirty" for him, but Billy and Harding, once the most cowardly of the inmates, are now transformed into heroes.

When the patients return to the dock with their catch, they have proven themselves. The loafers at the bait shop now look at them with a new respect and discuss fishing with them as they would among themselves. The patients have earned esteem in the eyes of others, and in their own eyes. But McMurphy looks "beat and worn out." On the way back to the hospital, he takes the group on a side trip, past his childhood home. He tells them about his first sexual experience, but the story has overtones of being a public performance, rather than a private reminiscence. McMurphy is offering himself to the others consciously now. He has to tell them how he became the way he is in order that they can become more like him. McMurphy is telling the story "for all of us to dream ourselves into"; he is making his private reality a public property, transforming his life into a myth for the others to participate in.

McMurphy is offering himself to the others consciously now. And as their self-assurance grows, he is becoming a product of their will. He seems to realize that in freeing them, he is dooming himself, but there is no longer any other alternative. No one else seems to notice, but the Chief sees McMurphy's face as "dreadfully tired and strained and *frantic*, like there wasn't enough time left for something he had to do."

PART 4

When the patients return from their fishing expedition, the Big Nurse is prepared to begin her counterattack. She believes that she has found McMurphy's weakness and she uses it to spread discontent among his followers. She has discovered that McMurphy has made a profit on the fishing trip; coupling this with his gambling with the patients, she tries to use this fact to persuade them that he is using them to take whatever he can. The device almost works, but Harding points out to the others that McMurphy is, after all, only human, and can be expected to look out for his own interests first. The other patients accept what Harding says and seem willing to forgive McMurphy, but McMurphy chooses this moment to make his mistake.

While the Big Nurse's warning is still fresh in the inmates' minds, McMurphy uses the Chief's new-found strength to win another bet from them. He holds the Chief to his promise to lift the control panel for him—but not until he has made a profitable wager on it with the other patients. The Chief is forced to go along with him, according to his promise, but he feels that he is being used to dupe the others. Afterward, he retreats to the shower room, where McMurphy follows him. The Chief tells McMurphy of the other patients' feelings about his winning all the time; McMurphy's response is: "Winning, for Christsakes. Hoo boy, winning." For the fact is, he has not won so much as he has lost. He has repeatedly put himself on the line, in order to bring the other patients back to life, and he is now forced into a hopeless situation. He must act again, risking his own safety, in order to preserve all he has gained for the others.

The occasion presents itself quickly. That afternoon, the patients are given a "cautionary cleansing" after their trip outside the hospital. George, the big Swede who had been captain of the fishing boat, resists the black boys' attempts to give him an enema, and McMurphy comes to his aid. He fights with the orderly Washington, but seems to hold back when he has the advantage, giving Washington the opportunity to call for help. By now, McMurphy seems to clearly understand what is to happen to him. He has been forced to defend George, against his own will. The Chief observes, "Everybody could hear the helpless, cornered despair in McMurphy's voice." And McMurphy is not fighting to win, but to be caught, so he can accept punishment on behalf of the group. Recognizing his own role in forcing McMurphy into this situation, by voicing the criticisms of the others, the Chief faces up to his responsibility and helps McMurphy defeat the black boys. But the outcome is inevitable; McMurphy has finally overstepped the bounds, and he and Chief Bromden are sent to Disturbed to await judgment.

For the first time in the novel, we are given a faint glimmer of humanity on the part of the hospital staff. The Japanese nurse on Disturbed criticizes Nurse Ratched's methods and agrees with McMurphy and the Chief. But she is powerless to help them since they are still, officially, patients of the Big Nurse.

When the Big Nurse confronts them, she gives McMurphy one last chance to admit he has been at fault — and to apologize. But it is too late for him to give in; he has to play the game to the end. So he and the Chief are sent to the Shock Shop, for Electro-Shock Therapy.

The biblical imagery is used again at this point: McMurphy is being symbolically crucified. He even jokes about it, referring to his head being "anointed" and asking for his crown of thorns. (These references are foreshadowed in the preceding scene, when one of the patients on Disturbed says "I wash my hands of the whole deal," a reference to Pilate's washing his hands after pronouncing sentence upon Christ.) McMurphy and the Chief are strapped to their "crosses" in the Shock Shop, and the voltage is applied.

Under the influence of the shock, the Chief has jumbled memories of his childhood and recites more details about his father's downfall. Among his confused ramblings is a passage which explicates further the title of the book: it is taken from a game his Indian grandmother used to play with him as a child:

> "Ting. Tingle, tingle, tremble toes, she's a good fisherman, catches hens, puts 'em inna pens...wire blier, limber lock, three geese inna flock . . . one flew east, one flew west, one flew over the cuckoo's nest . . . O-U-T spells out . . . goose swoops down and plucks *you* out."

This passage interconnects with symbols and images throughout the book. The "good fisherman" ties in with the fishing expedition, and Ellis's reference to being "fishers of men." But the "fisherman" in this case is apparently the Big Nurse; she "catches hens, puts 'em inna pens," just as Nurse Ratched encourages her charges to peck at one another like chickens in a barnyard. And the goose that "swoops down and plucks you out" is apparently the "bullgoose," McMurphy. The one he plucks out is Chief Bromden (". . . each of my fingernails looking up at her like a little face asking to be the *you* that the goose swoops down and plucks out.")

But for all the Chief's disconnected ramblings, this shock treatment is different from all the others the Chief has had. Before, he remained in a fog for days afterward; this time, he comes out of it quickly, with all his senses intact. And he is determined to resist the fog: "This time I had them beat." McMurphy has given him strength, and he refuses to give it up.

The Chief is given only one treatment before he is returned to the ward, but McMurphy remains behind to have three more. During this time, the Chief can see in McMurphy's face the same look he noticed on the way back from the fishing trip: McMurphy is being pushed to the limit of his endurance. When the Chief returns to the ward, he finds that he and McMurphy have become legendary heroes among the patients.

And no one is surprised when the Chief talks to them about McMurphy; the change in his behavior is taken for granted. All of them have changed. Billy is looking forward to the date he has made with Candy, when she is to sneak onto the ward at night and relieve him of his virginity. Harding has taken over McMurphy's role as a leader in his absence. All of the men are openly defying the Big Nurse.

A plan has been formulated for McMurphy's escape, the night of Billy's date. But McMurphy vetoes the plan when he returns, considering Billy's appointment more significant. After that is taken care of, he will consider escaping. The Big Nurse has brought him back to the ward because she sees that the legends about him are as much a threat as he is himself, and she attempts to keep him in line by threatening him with a lobotomy. But McMurphy still has his former self-assurance, though it is somewhat strained. He stands up to her, informing her that she cannot do anything to him as long as he behaves himself.

The reunion of Billy and Candy has been arranged by bribing the night orderly, an old Negro named Mr. Turkle. Candy and another whore, Sandy, are brought onto the ward through a window, and McMurphy is supposed to escape through this window later. But Candy and Sandy have brought along bottles of wine and vodka, the patients break into the nurses' station and steal some narcotic cough syrup, and Mr. Turkle produces some marijuana. The party gets out of hand, and McMurphy seems to lose all interest in keeping control as he gets drunk. Harding perceives what is happening. The patients are pushing their luck past the point of no return; they cannot escape punishment for this escapade. This seems, in fact, to be McMurphy's intention—to force the inmates into a situation in which they will have to defend themselves, rather than relying solely upon him. But the plan for his escape at the end of the party is abandoned and he is caught in the morning, along with the others.

Harding is the first to realize what has happened to McMurphy. During a discussion on the causes of insanity, he admits to McMurphy that the other patients were driven insane by their inability to cope with the world. But he points out that McMurphy, too, is now insane: he has been driven insane by being responsible for the others. This is the meaning of the weakness and fatigue which Chief Bromden has noted on McMurphy's face. He has been unable to withstand the pressures of his responsibility, and his own sanity has given way. All that is keeping him going now is the will of the group; his own will has withered away. McMurphy is no longer able to leave the hospital, just as the others have been unable to leave. His involuntary commitment has become voluntary; in strengthening the other patients, he has weakened himself to the point that he can no longer live outside the ward.

When the group is caught in the morning, the Big Nurse is at first unable to shake their self-confidence. But she quickly finds their weak spot and capitalizes upon them. Billy Bibbit has been caught with Candy. The Big Nurse breaks him down by threatening to tell his mother, who is an old friend of hers. And when Billy breaks, she predictably places the blame for his weakness squarely upon McMurphy. The Chief protests to him, "We don't blame you," but in the very fact of protesting, he has confirmed what Nurse Ratched has said. McMurphy has been betrayed by his followers.

But even Nurse Ratched did not count on the effect her plan has upon Billy. While left unattended in the office, overwhelmed by the guilt the Big Nurse has made him feel once again, he cuts his throat and kills himself. McMurphy is called upon to act one last time, to avenge Billy. But he is not acting for himself, but for all the other patients: "We couldn't stop him because we were the ones making him do it . . . it was our need that was making himself push slowly up from sitting . . . obeying orders beamed at him from forty masters. It was us that had been making him go on for weeks, keeping him standing long after his feet and legs had given out." McMurphy attacks Nurse Ratched, stripping her before the patients, exposing her weakness, her sexual identity. His attempt to strangle her is unsuccessful, but it is unnecessary. Her power has been dispelled by the disclosure of her body. She is no longer a threat to the patients.

McMurphy is taken away, and the Chief recognizes that he has fulfilled his purpose and is ready to die. But he is no longer needed. The patients now are able to fill his role themselves. Some of them leave the hospital, against medical advice; others transfer to other wards. Harding first takes over as dealer in the gambling games, then leaves the hospital as he has been planning, with his wife there to receive him. Only the Chief, Martini, and Scanlon are left when McMurphy is returned.

McMurphy has been lobotomized; his "castration" has been completed. But his legend lives on. The men refuse to recognize the "vegetable" that is brought back as McMurphy. The Chief knows it really is him and is determined to salvage what he can, rather than allow McMurphy to be used as an example of what happens to those who dare to defy authority. That night, when everyone else is apparently asleep, he smothers McMurphy. Scanlon, in the next bed, watches him do it, and the two plan the Chief's escape together. Chief Bromden lifts the control panel, as McMurphy taught him, and throws it through the window in a shower of glass, which "baptizes" the world outside (McMurphy's final blessing on the world he has just left). The Chief is free and on his own at last. "I been away a long time," he says, but now he is back, a new force of freedom in an overstructured world. We are left with the impression he is to carry on McMurphy's work, fighting the Combine.

On close reading, the conclusion of the book contains a curious series of ambiguities, which undercut its implicit optimism about the Chief's future. Before the Chief leaves, he tries on McMurphy's hat and finds it is too small for him. He has attained his full size and realizes now that he was really bigger than McMurphy. Symbolically, his rejection of the hat indicates that he does not need McMurphy any longer;

he is able to stand on his own. But it might also constitute a rejection of McMurphy's role—he will not be another McMurphy; he will be himself and fight his own battles.

There is also some indication that the Chief might not be successful in his flight from the hospital. In escaping, he chooses the route he had seen the dog take that other night, in the second section. Yet in his description of the dog, we were left with the image of him on a collision course with a car. Is the Chief simply setting out to be destroyed by the machines of the Combine, as the dog was destroyed by the car? For the defeat of the Big Nurse was, after all, only personal; the Combine still exists intact. These doubts lead back to the problem that the beginning of the book, in which the Chief's narration is clearly taking place inside the hospital at some time after McMurphy's death, cannot be totally dismissed as a lapse on the author's part. The ending is ambiguous, and the ambiguities cannot be fully resolved. The casual reader is left with the impression that McMurphy has succeeded and the Chief will survive. But a closer reading calls these conclusions into question, with the implication that the Combine is awaiting its chance to destroy Chief Bromden.

CHARACTER ANALYSES

RANDLE P. McMURPHY

Randle P. McMurphy is a wiry, red-haired, rude, "un-civilized" brawler. He is an ace con man, but at the same time curiously honest—for he never pretends to be anything other than what he is. It is this ability "to be himself" that sets him apart from the other inmates. He is his own man and has a free-dom which sets him apart from the frightened, repressed group of men who have placed themselves voluntarily under Nurse Ratched's authority.

Chief Bromden marvels that McMurphy has somehow been able to escape the influence of the Combine: he has never had the "machines" of civilization built into him. His behavior is "natural" in all senses of the word—spontaneous, unself-conscious, wild, and irrepressible. It is because of his ability to stand on his own that he becomes, at first uninten-tionally, the spokesman for the other inmates. He represents to them a clear alternative to the rigorous, structured repres-sion of society, represented by the Big Nurse and the Combine.

McMurphy is not insane when committed; he has come to the hospital as a ruse to escape work at the prison farm. At first, he is entirely self-centered; his rebellion against author-ity is merely an attempt to make his own life on the ward more comfortable. But his freedom becomes an example for the other inmates, and he becomes responsible for them. Ironically, he begins to lose his own freedom as he acts on the others' behalf, and, by the end of the novel, he has been driven insane by his efforts to make the others sane.

When McMurphy first discovers that, because he has been involuntarily committed, he cannot leave the hospital until released by the authorities, he attempts to become a model patient. But the other patients have come to depend upon him, and after Cheswick drowns himself and Harding is humiliated by his wife, McMurphy begins to understand his responsibility and to face up to it. He sets out to teach the others to be as self-sufficient as he is. But as he acts for them, he becomes their tool. As the patients become stronger, Mc-Murphy becomes weaker, until in the end he is no longer able to save himself.

As this transformation takes place in McMurphy's character, he is increasingly associated with Christ. At first there is merely a hint of this association — Ellis standing "crucified" against the wall of the ward, and the "cross" of the table in the Shock Shop. But this hint becomes stronger as the story progresses. McMurphy, like Christ, is "laying down his life that others might live": he is sacrificing himself for the benefit of the group, and in doing so, he loses his own free will. The Chief makes it clear at the end that McMurphy is not acting on his own in attacking the Big Nurse, but in accordance with the forty wills of the onlooking inmates.

Harding, in his last conversation with McMurphy, sums up what has happened: McMurphy is healing the others, but he has become insane in the process. In effect, he has ceased to be himself and is being forced to be what the others think he is. They can recognize themselves only through him, and he must continue to give them something to emulate.

In a sense, the Chief's killing of McMurphy is only an afterthought, for he has long since ceased to be himself, and now that he is a vegetable, he is no longer of any use to the inmates. He is already "dead"; the Chief is only confirming it.

NURSE RATCHED

The "Big Nurse" is never really characterized; she is more a symbol than a person. Chief Bromden's image of her has no correspondence with reality; she is part machine, part evil presence, able to blow herself up to superhuman proportions when aroused. She is a large, grey-haired former Army nurse, who insists upon running a tightly controlled ward. Everyone on her ward is under her control; even the doctor, who is theoretically in charge of the ward, was personally chosen by Nurse Ratched because his morphine addiction gives her a means of blackmailing him into submission. The "Therapeutic Community" she controls is built upon fear and suspicion. She keeps a log book for the patients to inform upon one another, and the "group therapy" meetings are sessions in which an inmate is selected to have his weaknesses publicly exposed. Her main purpose seems to be keeping her patients weak, in order that she can mold them into what she wants them to be—good, docile "rabbits" who can be sent back out to fill their places in society quietly.

The Big Nurse is generally depicted as huge, indomitable, and white (the color of sterility—sexual as well as sanitary). Her one weakness is her femininity, but she makes every attempt to conceal it. McMurphy continually emphasizes the size of her breasts, and when she is finally defeated, it is because McMurphy has torn open her uniform, exposing her sexuality.

In a way, the Big Nurse symbolizes what the author sees as wrong with women in modern society. She is characterized by McMurphy as a "ball-cutter"—a castrating woman, compulsively driven to destroy the masculinity of men. She is the prototype of Billy Bibbit's domineering mother and Harding's domineering wife. Most of the patients on the ward have been driven there by their relationships with women, and what they have fled to is a woman even more threatening than the ones from whom they were fleeing. What Nurse Ratched teaches her charges is not self-sufficiency, but submission.

CHIEF BROMDEN

We know more of the Chief's character than we do of the other characters in the story. As the narrator, he really tells us more about himself than about any of the others, even McMurphy or the Big Nurse. His mental state is characterized in a single stroke at the beginning of the novel: "They're out there." The Chief is a paranoid schizophrenic, ruled by his irrational fear of everything outside himself. He has been on the ward longer than any of the other patients, since the end of World War II (approximately fifteen years). His illness dates from childhood, when his tribe was destroyed to make way for a dam on their land near the Columbia River. Like many of the other patients, the cause of his downfall was a woman. It was his mother, Mary Louise Bromden, who betrayed the tribe and "shrunk" his father, turning him into an impotent, helpless alcoholic. As a mark of his shame, the Chief bears his white mother's name, rather than his father's. An institutionalized Indian, the Chief is an image of the subjection of wild nature to structured society.

The Chief is a large, powerful man, six feet seven inches tall, yet he believes he is small and weak. He is fully capable of hearing and comprehending what is going on, and of speaking—yet he poses as a deaf-mute. Throughout his life he has noticed that people paid no attention to him; they treated him as if he didn't exist. So he gradually gave up trying to communicate with the outside world and retreated into his subjective fantasies.

The Chief's madness manifests itself in his disarranged fantasies—the Nurse's ability to swell up to gigantic proportions, the vision of the butcher shop inside the dam, the machines in the walls, and the fog machine. When he is afraid, he fanticizes a fog into which he can escape. During his association with McMurphy, the fog gradually disappears and, along with it, other paranoid fantasies. He gradually becomes ready to speak again and to assume a normal life.

At the end of the novel, after McMurphy has been lobotomized, Chief Bromden assumes final responsibility. His killing of McMurphy and subsequent escape from the hospital indicate that his cure is complete. He has been "blown up" to full size by McMurphy, and he now is able to recognize how small McMurphy really was. When he tries on McMurphy's cap, it is too small to fit him. He has outgrown his need for McMurphy and is able to stand on his own.

THE PATIENTS

As a group, the patients on the ward are depicted as weak, spineless "rabbits," unable to assert themselves before the Big Nurse's authority. They have been driven to fear and suspect one another and to report on each other's weaknesses in order to gain favor with Nurse Ratched. She goads them into attacking each other and publicly confessing their illness. As individuals, most of the patients are more caricature than character; they are one-dimensional "cartoon" figures, lacking any real depth. Their only distinctive features are the symptoms of their particular diseases. There are, however, two exceptions to this rule — Harding and Billy Bibbit.

DALE HARDING

Harding is a weak, effeminate man who has been dominated by his wife. He is ashamed of his effeminacy, but unable to control his white, graceful hands. Yet Harding is probably the strongest of the patients, with the exception of McMurphy. He is the leader of the Patients' Council and among the first to follow McMurphy. His cure is gradual, but by the time McMurphy is sent to Disturbed for fighting with the black boys, Harding is able to take his place, dealing blackjack and speaking for the men. Yet he refuses to escape from the ward when the opportunity presents itself at the party; he insists upon leaving as he has planned, with his wife coming to get him. This is the only way in which he can demonstrate his ability to control her; it is a mark of the extent to which he has been cured.

BILLY BIBBIT

Billy is the shyest and most repressed member of the group. He is thirty-one years old, yet he still acts like an adolescent. His whole life has been dominated by his mother, who refuses to treat him like an adult. In the hospital, this same role is assumed by his mother's friend, Nurse Ratched. McMurphy almost succeeds in leading Billy to manhood: he does arrange for Billy to lose his virginity with the whore Candy. And Billy does, briefly, defy the Big Nurse. But the Nurse capitalizes upon Billy's weakness, shaming him with the threat of reporting his escapade to his mother. And Billy, still unable to defend his manhood, cuts his throat.

Special Topics

THE TITLE

The title of the book is clearly allegorical in its intent. The "cuckoo's nest" is the hospital, and the one who "flew over" it is McMurphy. The full nursery rhyme from which the title is taken is quoted in Part 4 by the Chief, as he remembers his childhood while awaking from a shock treatment. The rhyme was part of a childhood game played with him by his Indian grandmother:

> Ting. Tingle, tingle, tremble toes, she's a good fisherman, catches hens, puts 'em inna pens . . . wire blier, limber lock, three geese inna flock . . . one flew east, one flew west, one flew over the cuckoo's nest . . . O-U-T spells out . . . goose swoops down and plucks you *out*.

The goose who flies over the cuckoo's nest is McMurphy, the "chief bullgoose loony"; the one he "plucks out" is the Chief, who escapes at the end of the novel, following McMurphy's teaching. The goose is also the leader of the flight of wild geese, silhouetted against the moon above the asylum in the shape of a cross, foreshadowing McMurphy's "crucifixion" in the Shock Shop. "Tingle, tingle, tremble toes" is clearly the Big Nurse, who catches the inmates like hens and encourages them to peck one another to death in the "pen" of the ward, where they are kept locked in. That she is "a good fisherman," a "fisher of men," recalls McMurphy's fishing expedition and its symbolic overtones linking McMurphy with Christ, but her purpose is to imprison, rather than to liberate, her catch.

POINT OF VIEW

Kesey himself considers point of view the key to this book, and it is certainly the case that the book is more effective because of its narration. The fact that the narrator is insane frees the author from presenting an objective account of the action, for much of the plot takes place in the narrator's distorted subconscious. Kesey suggests that the choice of an Indian as narrator may have come from the association of Indians with peyote, a drug produced from a cactus by the Indians of the southwestern United States. It is at least obvious that the choice of narrator corresponds with Kesey's interest in states of altered consciousness, whether by madness or by drugs. It is his belief that the mind of a madman, like that of one who is high on drugs, is released from the preconceptions of society and is able to respond naturally and immediately to the moment. This state of altered perception in the book is frequently poetic in its method, seizing upon images as symbols of reality.

If the reader approaches the book as a literal rendering of a story, however, the narration is bound to cause him problems. The Chief is not consistent with reality; he is sometimes not even consistent with himself. For instance, the first section of Part 1 is an introduction to the story, presumably being told by the Chief after McMurphy is dead. He is deep in his paranoia, attempting to hide in the fog on the ward from the black boys and the Big Nurse. Yet at the end of the book we are told that immediately after killing McMurphy, his illness cured, the Chief breaks out of the hospital and escapes. Are we to assume that he was recaptured and brought back, or is it a major inconsistency in the narration? What the Chief says in introducing his story is a clue:

> I been silent so long now it's gonna roar out of me like floodwaters and you think the guy telling this is ranting and raving my *God*; you think this is too horrible to have really happened, this is too awful to be the truth! But, please. It's still hard for me to have a clear mind thinking on it. But it's the truth even if it didn't happen.

"It's the truth even it if didn't happen": what the reader is to expect is not a literal accounting of factual events, but another form of truth. It is the truth of poetic experience, of myth — the epic encounter of superhuman forces (represented by Mc-Murphy and the Big Nurse) acted out on a symbolic battle-ground.

Nor does the action of the novel always take place at the literal level. One prime example is the Chief's dream-vision of the mechanized butcher shop under the dam. The image of the dam is clearly drawn from the Chief's bitter memories of childhood, when his tribe was moved to make way for a hydro-electric dam on the Columbia River. And the Chief's phobia about machines and electricity is focused in this passage, in which human corpses are being moved about on mechanized meathooks. Yet the passage is more than a vision: the Chief awakes to find that Old Blastic, one of the vegetables, has died during the night. It was his corpse which the workers under the dam had come to claim. His nightmare has not come true; it *was* true, with the truth of a symbolic world which touches upon reality.

As the book progresses, we have fewer and fewer of these visions. The fog machine, which obscured the action of some passages while the Chief hid from his persecutors, fades away as the Chief's strength grows. And as he regains the will to communicate, the Chief becomes more and more an active part of the story: he no longer is content to communicate what he saw, or envisioned, to himself alone; he wants to communicate what he *did*, to others besides himself. The narration becomes more and more coherent and closer to everyday reality as the Chief regains his sanity. And, in effect, the story is "demythologized" at the end. With the Big Nurse put in her place, and McMurphy dead, the Chief prepares to escape. But, first, he must try on the hat of his hero, the "giant" McMurphy. It is too small for him. The symbols have been returned to the mundane world of the real. But this is not to say they were never anything more: "It's the truth even if it didn't happen."

THE MACHINE

Chief Bromden's fantasies are dominated by machines, and so, consequently, are the images of the novel. The machine is seen as wholly inimical, the opposite of everything that is natural. The "Combine," the name the Chief gives to organized society, is a term for a threshing machine, used for mowing down and harvesting wheat. When the Big Nurse is angry, she is compared to a diesel truck run amok, smelling of burning oil. The machines in the Shock Shop are used to punish patients who step out of line; the fog machine is turned on to isolate and confuse the patients; and machines are installed in the walls of the ward, and even in the patients themselves, to keep everything running according to the Combine's plan.

The machines are the images of the mechanical order which the Combine is attempting to impose upon society; yet, paradoxically, they are instruments of chaos, associated with destruction and confusion. When the inmates travel outside the hospital with McMurphy—Chief Bromden for the first time in fifteen years—they notice the mechanical conformity that has been imposed upon the world during their absence:

> Or things like five thousand houses punched out identical by a machine and strung across the hills outside of town, so fresh from the factory they're still linked together like sausages . . . there were five thousand kids in green corduroy pants and white shirts under green pullover sweaters playing crack-the-whip across an acre of crushed gravel. The line popped and twisted and jerked like a snake, and every crack popped a little kid off the end, sent him rolling up against the fence like a tumbleweed. Every crack. And it was always the same little kid, over and over.

The absolute conformity of the machine is not order, but chaos replicated over and over again with monotonous regularity.

And Harding's vision of society overthrown by the inmates being let out repeats the same motif: a babbling schizophrenic running a wrecking machine, the force of chaos released upon itself. This is nothing more than the same image reversed, for the opposite of society's order is not chaos, but the order of Nature, which is what McMurphy represents.

RELIGIOUS IMAGERY

Kesey uses images associated with Christ and his crucifixion sparingly throughout the early parts of the book, but increases them in the final chapters, when the confrontation with the Big Nurse is deepening and McMurphy's martyrdom becomes imminent. The first such image is of the Chronic patient Ellis, whose mind has been ravaged by repeated shock treatments, standing "crucified," his arms outspread against the wall. Ellis's stance is reflected in the shape of the table used for Electro-Shock Therapy: it is shaped like a cross and the patient is strapped to it, like Christ nailed to the cross.

The image of Ellis standing against the wall recurs throughout the book, but is not developed further until the scene immediately preceding the fishing expedition. As the patients are leaving the ward, Ellis pulls his hand from the wall, shakes Billy Bibbit's hand, and tells him to be a "fisher of men" — a phrase used by Christ to his disciples, referring to the winning of converts to his cause. And, in effect, the fishing trip is the conversion — even the "salvation," if you will — of McMurphy's followers, who, like Christ's disciples, are twelve in number. It is on the sea that the inmates first learn to stand firm in their own identities; they learn how, like McMurphy, to be themselves. It is for this reason that during the storm at sea, McMurphy is content to stay in the background and let others — Harding, Billy Bibbit, and George — be the "heroes" who face the storm without life jackets. They are "proving" themselves.

After McMurphy and the Chief fight the black boys, they are taken to Disturbed, where they are confronted by a patient who says, "I wash my hands of the whole deal." The reference here is to Pontius Pilate, who condemned Christ to be crucified, washing his hands after the trial. "To wash one's hands of something" is to refuse to participate in the guilt associated with it.

As McMurphy and the Chief are awaiting their shock treatments, another patient is crying, saying, "It's my cross, thank you Lord, it's all I got, thank you Lord." And as McMurphy prepares to take his treatment, the references multiply:

> Climbs on the table without any help and spreads his arms out to fit the shadow. A switch snaps the clasps on his wrists, ankles, clamping him into the shadow.
>
> . . . .
>
> They put the graphite salve on his temples. "What is it?" he says. "Conductant," the technician says. "Anointest my head with conductant. Do I get a crown of thorns?"
>
> . . . .
>
> Put on those things like headphones, crown of silver thorns over the graphite at his temples. They try to hush his singing with a piece of rubber hose for him to bite on.

The preparations for the shock treatment all parallel the crucifixion; even the rubber hose for him to bite, which is like the sponge soaked in vinegar which a Roman soldier held on a stick for Christ to suck while on the cross.

The parallel between McMurphy and Christ is obvious: both "gave their lives that others might live." But this parallel should not be pushed too far; the martyrdoms of the meek, mild, gentle celibate and the lusty, brawling con man have quite different meanings. Christ died to redeem the sins of the individual; McMurphy's death is not to save the other patients from their own sins, but from society's sins against them. As Christ's death was a triumph of the soul, McMurphy's is a triumph of the flesh: he has relieved them of the guilt they have been taught by women to feel over their natural sexual urges. And he has prepared them for what Kesey seems to consider their rightful place in society—dominating women, rather than being dominated by them.

THE ROLE OF WOMEN

Women in the book are of two sorts—"ball-cutters" like the Big Nurse, who are intent upon dominating men by depriving them of their masculinity, and whores like Candy and Sandy, who are submissive toward men and intent upon giving them pleasure. The fact that there is no middle ground between these extremes is typical of the book, with its polarities of good and evil, mechanical and natural, civilized and wild, etc. The intent of this dichotomy is not to denigrate women (though this is, undeniably, one of the side effects); it is simply a part of the mythic system Kesey develops in the book. One of the cardinal virtues in McMurphy's world is masculinity, which is associated with nature, spontaneity, and rebellion against the social organization of the Combine. Women who acquiesce in a man's masculinity, like Candy, are good; those who oppose it, like Nurse Ratched, are evil. Thus we have the dominant female figures of the book: Nurse Ratched, Billy's mother, Harding's wife, and the Chief's mother. The last of these is the one we know the most about, apart from the Big Nurse, who we see only on the ward. Through Mrs. Bromden, we see how the "castration" of both husband and son, works.

It was through Mrs. Bromden that the Combine first gained rights to the Indian land on the Columbia where the dam was built. Two white men and a woman had come to speak with the Chief's father, but upon learning that his wife was a white woman, they decided to approach the matter to her. We are never given details of the deal that was made, but apparently they appealed to her desire to return to "civilization," to move into town. And once she had asserted her power, she began to "grow" (in the Chief's mind, power and size are inextricably linked—hence, the "Big Nurse"). Explaining this to McMurphy, he says, "A guy at the carnival looked her over and says five feet nine and weight a hundred and thirty pounds, but that was because he'd just *saw* her. She got bigger all the time.

As Mrs. Bromden grew, her husband began to "shrink" in size, and she came more and more to dominate him. And her son, who had already learned that he was invisible to white people, never stood a chance of countering her influence. And so it came to be that, like his father, he had only one name—but the name was his mother's.

Mama's name was Bromden. Still is Bromden. Papa said he was born with only one name, born smack into it the way a calf drops out in a spread blanket when the cow insists on standing up. Tee Ah Millatoona, the Pine-That-Stands-Tallest-on-the-Mountain, and I'm the biggest by God Injun in the state of Oregon and probly California and Idaho. Born right into it.

You're the biggest by God fool if you think that a good Christian woman takes on a name like Tee Ah Millatoona. You were born into a name, so okay, I'm born into a name. Bromden. Mary Louise Bromden.

And when we move into town, Papa says, that name makes gettin' that Social Security card a lot easier.

The mother's name is an image of the father's subjection, a mark of his "civilization" in the sacrifice of his pride and self-sufficiency. As his father was born into his Indian name, Chief Bromden was born into his mother's, and as the name and what is symbolized drove his father to alcoholism and death, it drove the son to the hospital.

Nurse Ratched is to the Chief a surrogate of his mother, as she is to Billy Bibbit, and a surrogate wife to Harding. She is the living symbol of their disease, as the archetype of the repressive forces in society which drove them insane. This is why she must be defeated by McMurphy before the other inmates can have their masculinity back.

REVIEW QUESTIONS

1. What are the strengths and weaknesses of Kesey's use of Chief Bromden as narrator in the book? To what extent does the Chief's madness interfere with the reader's understanding of what is actually happening? To what extent do his visions symbolically reinforce the themes of the novel?

2. One of Kesey's main goals in the novel is exploring other modes of consciousness. How successful is he in establishing their validity?

3. Consider Nurse Ratched as a character, rather than a symbol. How much do we really know about her personality?

4. Consider the "fictional present" established by the author at the beginning of the first chapter, the moment in time from which the story is being told. How do you justify its conflict with the conclusion of the novel?

5. Discuss McMurphy as a Christ figure. In what ways does he fit the role? In what ways does he not fit?

6. Trace references to machines throughout the book. Does the frequency with which they are mentioned as threatening correspond in any way with the Chief's mental states?

7. Given the role of women in the book, speculate about the author's opinions on the Women's Liberation movement.

8. If you have read Melville's *Moby-Dick*, discuss the ways in which Kesey uses allusions to the novel.

9. In what ways does Kesey use the setting of the novel as a vehicle for social satire?

10. Toward the end of the novel, Harding implicitly compares McMurphy with the Lone Ranger, saying "Who was that masked man?" Compare McMurphy with comic-strip, radio, and television "superheroes."

11. Who is the real protagonist of the novel—McMurphy or Chief Bromden?

SELECTED BIBLIOGRAPHY

WORKS BY KESEY:

One Flew Over the Cuckoo's Nest, 1962.

Sometimes a Great Notion, 1964.

Ken Kesey's Garage Sale, 1973.

CRITICISM AND COMMENTARY

Fiedler, Leslie A. *The Return of the Vanishing American.* New York, 1968.

Klein, Marcus (ed.) *The American Novel Since World War II.* Greenwich, Conn., 1969.

Pratt, John C. (ed.) *One Flew Over the Cuckoo's Nest: Text and Criticism.* New York, 1973.

Wolfe, Tom. *The Electric Kool-Aid Acid Test.* New York, 1968.

ARTICLES

Blessing, Richard. "The Moving Target: Ken Kesey's Evolving Hero," *Journal of Popular Culture* 4: 615-27.

Hoge, James O. "Psychedelic Stimulation and the Creative Imagination: The Case of Ken Kesey." *Southern Humanities Review* 6: 381-91.

Sherwood, Terry. *"One Flew Over the Cuckoo's Nest* and the Comic Strip." *Critique* 13: 96-109.

Sutherland, Janet. "A Defense of Ken Kesey's One Flew Over the Cuckoo's Nest." *English Journal* 61: 28-36.

Waldmeier, Joseph J. "Two Novelists of the Absurd: Heller and Kesey." *Wisconsin Studies in American Literature* 5: 192-204.

NOTES

Your Guides to Successful Test Preparation.

Cliffs Test Preparation Guides
• *Complete* • *Concise* • *Functional* • *In-depth*

ficient preparation means better test scores. Go with the experts and use *iffs Test Preparation Guides.* They focus on helping you know what to expect •m each test, and their test-taking techniques have been proven in class-om programs nationwide. Recommended for individual use or as a part a formal test preparation program.

ilisher's ISBN Prefix 0-8220

ty.	ISBN	Title	Price	Qty.	ISBN	Title	Price
	2078-5	ACT	8.95		2044-0	Police Sergeant Exam	9.95
	2069-6	CBEST	8.95		2047-5	Police Officer Exam	14.95
	2056-4	CLAST	9.95		2049-1	Police Management Exam	17.95
	2071-8	ELM Review	8.95		2076-9	Praxis I: PPST	9.95
	2077-7	GED	11.95		2017-3	Praxis II: NTE Core Battery	14.95
	2061-0	GMAT	9.95		2074-2	SAT*	9.95
	2073-4	GRE	9.95		2325-3	SAT II*	14.95
	2066-1	LSAT	9.95		2072-6	TASP	8.95
	2046-7	MAT	12.95		2079-3	TOEFL w/cassettes	29.95
	2033-5	Math Review	8.95		2080-7	TOEFL Adv. Prac. (w/cass.)	24.95
	2048-3	MSAT	24.95		2034-3	Verbal Review	7.95
	2020-3	Memory Power for Exams	5.95		2043-2	Writing Proficiency Exam	8.95

Prices subject to change without notice.

ilable at your ıksellers, or send ; form with your •ck or money order Cliffs Notes, Inc., •. Box 80728, coln, NE 68501 ɔ://www.cliffs.com

Cliffs
NOTES